If language at the same time shapes and distorts our ideas and emotions, how do we communicate love?

If language at the same time shapes and distorts our ideas and emotions, how do we communicate love?

poems by Aiden Shaw

the bad press   manchester

All poems copyright Aiden Shaw 1996
All rights reserved
Published 1996 by The Bad Press
PO Box 76, Manchester M21 8HJ

ISBN 0-9517233-3-2 softcover
ISBN 0-9517233-4-0 hardcover

A limited edition of 250 hardcover copies
Signed by Aiden Shaw and Pierre et Gilles

British Library Cataloguing-in-Publication-Data
A catalogue record for this book is available
from the British Library

Softback Artwork - Aiden Shaw
Softback photograph - James and James
Hardback photograph - Pierre et Gilles
Frontspiece photograph - Jorge Quiroz
Typeset by Print North West Limited
Design - Robert Cochrane

CONTENTS

My heart muscle is hard	9
You think that you're being kissed	12
I love to look at a man	13
Melting	14
Being taught to have faith...	15
A man that I have sex with...	16
Somebody once asked me...	17
The ideal	18
Never before have I seen a mouth...	19
The neighbours dog is a big fucker	20
When I was wanking	22
I once kissed a boy who was dead	23
If you die before I do	24
I notice changes in my body	25
A constant reminder	27
Will you help me?	29
How would that seem now?	31
Might the God...	32
This punter played some opera	33
I stand and look in the mirror	34
I once saw a large white bird	35
I lived my fantasies	36
Snow Love	37

Also by Aiden Shaw
a novel
Brutal (Millivres)

This is dedicated to
All the friends who've been false to me
All the grown ups who misguided me
All the lovers that hated me
All the teachers that tried to trick me
All the officials who've lied
All the religions that abused my faith
All the punters who cheated me
All the people who've put me down or enjoyed embarrassing me
To all the things in my life that ever made sad
And made me react

My heart muscle is hard.
Push your hand inside my arse,
Take hold of my heart in between your fingers,
Pull it from within,
Out into this world,
And beat it.
Beat it until it is tender.
Tender enough to care.
Caring enough to share.
Pummel it if you have to,
Until it softens,
And I am of use again.

Just a look from you
To know you noticed me
This is all I'd want

No
Because then
That smile that you have
I'd want that used on me
But this is all I'd want

No
Because then
This would probably make me feel so much
I'd want to sit close to you
And become a part of whatever you were doing
This would satisfy me

No
I guess it wouldn't
Because how could I be so close to you
Watching you move
Smelling your smell
And not want to kiss your face
And I would have to be a fool not to want to spend more than a little time with you
But if we did
I think then I would be happy
Surely I would
If you gave me this

No
Because then there would be one thing more that I would want from you
I would want your all
Your everything
But I know this is so much to give
So I'll just catch a look
And this will be enough
At least you noticed me

You think that you're being kissed
But I'm talking to you.
My lips are mouthing words
Not slipping, meaning nothing.
You can't hear me because my voice is so so quiet
So much so that the sound doesn't even leave my head
Although I'm thinking loudly what I feel
All you hear is the sound of kisses
My breathing and my sighs.

When you were asleep I couldn't help it
I said things
You, me, us, things.
Surely there's only so much I can think before it comes out anyway
Before it shows itself somehow
With some kind of noise
A language of noise
In sounds made by kisses
My breathing and my sighs.

In truth I want you to hear
Stuff that isn't spoken
Words are needless anyway
If you know what to make of my kissing, breathing, sighs.

I love to look at a man
More than this I love to smell a man
More than this I love to kiss a man
More than this I love to feel a man's hard cock against me
More than this I love to suck a man's hard cock
More than this I love to make a man cum
More than this I love to swallow a man's cum
More than this I love to fuck with a man and cum in his
  arse or him cum in mine.
More than this I love life
More than this I love to look at man
More than this I love to smell a man
repeat and fade

Melting,
Sweat dribbling down my neck.
Daydreaming.
The story of the boy with the butterflies fluttering on his crotch.
Their colors so vivid in the sunlight,
The boy so naked,
The explosion of his first load through the flower-like cluster.
Daydreaming.
Light pin pricks,
I'm bound and gaged,
Blind folded,
Not knowing where I will feel next.
Waiting.
Daydreaming.
A thousand deer-flies
Golden green
Glistening veined wings,
Iridescent,
Shelled bodies like drops of fresh blood,
Dipping into me
One by one,
Filling themselves up,
Drinking,
Hovering,
Then bursting through my skin for more.
From a distance this mist of insects is just one thing,
But I can see them clearly,
Kissing me,
Pricking me.
I could die here on this grass.
How many times could I be kissed before I die?

Being taught to have faith
I learned to have none
So all love in my life became a decision

Then came you
And when you didn't sleep at night
It bothered me
And when we argued
I didn't sleep at night
Slowly the ability to have faith came back
Through believing in you

Trying to get through
The barriers
The nonsense
And the madness
I understand now
That I was ruined
Without faith

A man that I have sex with is lying in front of me,
He is strong and kind.
Sometimes he ties me on his bed
So that I cannot move,
I like this.
Sometimes he likes me to cover his body in clothes pegs which pinch his skin,
Starting with his nipples and then his cock.
He is older than me so his skin is not so tight,
I like this.
When I have covered his body as much as I can he looks really good,
More colourful than a peacock
And less proud,
With something that makes me want to love him as much as I can.
It's like I want to help him,
But I know he's stronger and can help me more.
When I see him like this
I want to worship him,
And hurt him,
Because I know that's what he wants.
When I hurt him too much that's when we both know it's even better.

Somebody once asked me. 'How much do you love me?'
I said,'This much,'
And stretched out my arms as far as they would go.
'Is that all?' they said.
So I stretched further, expanding my chest and reaching as
  far as I could.
But still this wasn't enough for them.
Once again I stretched,
This time so far back that my knuckles met behind me.
At this point my skin began to split,
My ribs began to crack,
My chest tore open,
My heart burst out
And fell to the floor.
We both looked at it as it became cooler and cooler
And more still and more still
Until finally it was cold and dead.
Then a crowd of strangers appeared
And one by one they approached.
But because they didn't recognize my heart
They trampled over it.
I have learnt from this
Never to show somebody how much I love them.

The ideal

Being with someone I love
And being so completely comfortable
That I can be by myself with them
We can be alone
But have the company of each other together

The reality

Being with somebody,
Possibly a lover or a friend
Not even thinking of someone else
But feeling lonely in their arms
Feeling separate and not together with them
And putting up with this

Never before have I seen a mouth that I would so eagerly drink from
I would have swallowed his spit
Just knowing that it came from those lips
I would have loved to have inside me
Anything that came from his body
His sweat
His cum
His blood
Even his tears
Just because they were his

The neighbour's dog is a big fucker
His tight black coat moves over his muscles like a wet-suit
I watch him
He's inside and I'm outside
I know he's alone in there
So it's just him and me
He starts to get angry
Pounding against the window
Like he wants to mash me
Kill me

I'm drawn closer
From here his face appears to be scarred across the cheek
Mean not ugly
Closer still I can feel the glass throb as he thrashes against it
Unbuttoning my jeans I pull them down over my now
   swelling dick
I press up against this monster
And can feel the heat from his muscles
As he thrashes against my balls
Driving a thud through to my arse making me want to cum

He crashes
I jolt away from the window
But return in seconds
Glued to this heaving
Mass of meat
He scares the shit out of me
Bringing me closer
His huge shoulders
Hammering me

Closer still
He'd gnaw my balls off
Now squashed hot against his face
He looks into my eyes
He knows what's going on
Fuck it's too much
I can't hold back

I shoot
He starts to lick the window
My hot cum running down over his face
He can't hurt me

When I was wanking
I thought of a beautiful man that I know,
After a couple of strokes
I remembered that he was dead.
I was confused,
I didn't know whether I was honouring him or abusing him.
It was as though I were trapping him in a physical world.

I once kissed a boy who was dead,
His lips were tinged with purple,
His eyes showed no reaction.
I took off my clothes and lay down,
He was so cold that I felt cold beside him,
He gave me nothing,
This made me feel dead as well.
I fucked this boy.
Still he did not respond.
What is the point of this I thought,
Even if this is just for me,
Without his response there's no joy.
When I thought I was finished he turned to me and said,
'My lips are tinged with purple
They are bruised beyond belief,
I've been lying here such a long time that my skin is very cold,
My eyes show no reaction
Because I do not want to hurt you
Or see what could hurt me,
How can I give a response
When all you did was fuck me!

If you die before I do
Then all my feelings will slip from me.
I will gather these splinters and lay them on the ground,
These will make a copy of you.
I will find tiny flowers of every colour to shroud your body
Then in your bed
I will stick these little bits of wreath all over you.
I will kiss each one
A million kisses probably.
On your lips I will put pink reddish petals,
I will remember the colour they were.
Under your eyes I will kiss and stick lavender hues.
I will find every shade of any bloom that could show how dear
  you are
And how good looking you were.
Maybe they might smell as sweet to me as well.
I will remember everything about you.
I will kiss your unfeeling lips,
This would be heavenly for me.
I will imagine everything about you.
I will touch you with feelings still so alive in me.
I will put my burning tongue in your tasty frigid mouth
Holding your jaw apart with my fingers.
I will feel passion.
I will lie on top of you
So that my heart might effect you so much
That it might bring your's back to beating
Then beat.

I notice changes in my body
Little by little
The skin on my face is getting more lines
And although my teenage spots went away
The pit marks probably never will
My ribs have little dry dots on them
These start at my hip and come up under my arm
I have athlete's foot
I have eczema
My doctor say's my skin complaints are probably not related to HIV
I do have the HIV virus
Which may or may not be causing my diarrhea
My constant migraine headaches
And my general tiredness
Some days I feel fit and well and full of life
Some days I don't feel any of these
My mouth smells
And my teeth are rotting
Slowly but surely
Just like everyone else's
And just like everyone else there's usually something wrong with me
A cold or flu
Or a stomach ache
I have a verruca on each of my feet
I have two warts on my finger tips
I sound like a monster
But I am not
I am selfish sometimes
And don't care about things
People seem odd and different to me

I can't relate to what others want in life
Or the ways they want to get it
I can be unsocial
And dismissive
One-sided
And sure
I am getting older
Maybe I should lie
And not see my life for what it is

A constant reminder
Of a life near over,
Of a half lived life,
Humbling,
Reminding,
Mocking,
Reminding,
Instilling fear
And reminding how nearly not mine life could be,
How unspecial it can be,
How taken away
And laughed at it will be,
Always reminded,
Not of the closeness of friends
But of the closeness of not being in their lives.
Little things going wrong
And all caves in.
The vibrant, confident, positive full of life
Way of life
Gives way to the scared,
The allowing
The taking its course
Of the coarsest
And evil self-surrender.
Relentlessly reminded of me not being.
The humiliating,
Loathsome
Reminder

Instilling a more bitter self
Unpure of love and kindness,
Because there's nothing left
No good life to live
No strength to make it good.
Just dim moments,
Ugly half-recognitions of what had been,
But still a constant reminder,
Constantly reminding
Of the constant drawing nearer to the
Life is over.
From the pathetic attempt at a life full lived
I become the reminder
To others of their lives near end.

'Will you help me?'
'Of course what is it?'
'It's something special.'
'What is it?'
'I know it's a lot to ask but that's why I chose you.'
'Just ask, there's no need to worry,
 You know I'd do anything for you.'
'In that case, how sweet can you be to me.'
'Too sweet.'
'Will you give me a kiss?'
'You know I love to kiss you.'
'Will you hold my nose?'
'What for, I don't understand.'
'So that when you kiss me I can't breath.'
'Don't joke, I could never hurt you.'
'I don't want you to hurt me. I'm asking you to help me stop hurting.'
'I can't believe what you're saying.'
'It's plain and simple, I want you to kiss me until I die. I'm weak, I'm sore and you know about all the other stuff.'
'What other stuff?'
'The how much I love you stuff.'
'Okay, I know what you want and I know why, and I can see why you're asking me but surely this is wrong.
'Wrong or right, I can't walk, I can't stand up, I can't eat, I can't shit by myself. I can't live by myself, do you know what I mean, can you imagine how this feels.'
'You don't have to do anything by yourself, you've got me.'
'This just isn't how I want it to be.'
'But what about me?'
'You'll say you can't live without me, but you can and you will. Now how strong will you be for me?'
'Of course I'll do it, what choice do I have, I love you.'

How would that seem now?
That all consuming
All forgiving
Always
In all ways kind
Safe
Sanctuary
Gently breathing
Mother's breath
Hands and head protecting

How would that seem now?
Being used to adult loves
Of the cruel
Of strangers who deceive with lovely looks and smiles
She wouldn't have let them near.
How can I protect myself without that
Without her?

I do have love now
But her's was even more than this.
What she gave was more ground like than concrete.
There was never a thought to that love not being there
And she gave and gave and I took.
There was never a need to question
When so young,
So aimless,
She guided,
She was all forgiving.
She was the real God for so much of my life.

Might the God which some of us believe in ban me from it's heaven and it's hell.
Might the soul which governs each living body cry itself out for me.
Might all women and all men laugh at me.
Might my own heart within me disperse as though it were just any other organ.
Might the child which could have come from me lie still.
Might the friends which could have cherished me, not care.
If I do not feel in this life.
If I do not love,
Might I care?

This punter played some opera whilst he licked my arse,
Sucked my arse,
Wallowed in my cum,
Using it to lubricate his circumcised wanking.
When he was finished I asked if I could take a shower.
This man's cat was old and incontinent.
There were two lots of shit beside the bathtub.
I stepped over them.
He said,
'You're not bothered are you.?'
I thought,
I am.
Then I showered thinking how cat shit smelt different to
 punter shit.
Now I'm with my baby it's me who's licking, sucking and
 wallowing.
Again I think of shit and how different it smells when
 fucking with passion.

I stand and look in the mirror,
My face is covered in cum.
I wash in the sink,
The water becomes stringy.
I am not washing away the act, just the evidence.

I stand and look in the mirror,
My face is covered in shit.
I wash in the sink,
The water becomes yellowy-brown.
I am not washing away the act, just the evidence.

I once saw a large white bird collapse and begin to die
Its powerful wings wrinkled clumsily around its warm
Then cooler body
How embarrassing
The loss of control
The loss of grace

Now in front of me
Thick white fingers
Try to cover a face crumbling with shame
Fingers pouring over water
On a face

I
Like the creator of all things
Of the large white bird
Of the fumbling fingers
I can bring back to life
With the right gesture
Everything that was destroyed

How powerful am I?

I lived my fantasies
I became my fantasy
Until what I had been became my fantasy

Snow Love

If I said I'd been here thousands of years
You might want to stop and lend me your ears.
I'll tell you something that not many know,
The warming tale of how snow-love can grow.

I once had some friends
Made up out of snow
From the top of their hats
To the tip of their toes,
With big snow-hearts that were able to shine,
Snow-thoughts,
Snow-feelings,
And even snow-minds.

The two of this tale first laid sooty eyes
Amidst cool flurry and blushing sighs.
Neither had felt like this before
In all their years and even more.
And snow's been around for ever you know,
Since there's been weather
There's always been snow.
They reached out with boldness
Their fingers of chill,
So much coldness,
Perfect still.
A shiver ran down and up their spines,
A spark of ice in two curved lines.
This means sheer-love to any snow-pair,

So as they kissed, good travelled through air.
Two souls mix and smile sometimes.
Happy lips fix with a crack of chimes.
Snugly welding, their round heads span.
This is how their thing began.

Snow-hearts warming every breath
Changing them to slushy wet.
Tears of melt start to fall
From icy faces hands and all,
Clumsy bodies trickling drip,
What will become of this lip to lip?
This was only once a kiss,
But soon might end as cloud and mist.
A puddle waits around their feet,
A muddled sleet which was their feet.
This is not sad, they're not like us.
It's snow-love so let's not make a fuss.
Suddenly when see-through thin
They change outside but not within.
Now their love was all combined,
As liquid mixed
They felt divine.
Water,
With water,
The very same thing,
For us this is but imagining.

Through this winter's frosty air
Comes sun to warm this heart-affair.
Then blazing heat begins to dry,
And vaporize them into sky.
The term they use is lessening,
Until there's nothing,
Not a thing.

Now as air they become aware
Of smells that are hanging there,
Fresh mown grass at summer dusk,
Bonfires burning,
Arousing musk,
Farm-yards,
Babies,
Christmas trees
All stream by like whales at sea.

Shape is what they discover next
Two kinds in fact it's quite complex.
First there's things that float on by
Like glassy wings from a fly,
Butter-cup dust from petals buffed,
Gas stuffed balloons fully puffed,
Fuzzy fluff off honey bees,
Aimless crispy-branchless leaves.

Next there's space around all things
Like the shape which defines a goblin queen,
A skunk,
A punk, or an old man's spleen.
The squarey outline of a Spanish villa
And that long thin tube of a caterpillar.
Forms like these and many more
Float in, around and out of doors.

Noise also fills the air,
By now there's hardly room to spare.
The toot-come-warble of a black-bird's song,
Motor-bike revs that last too long.
Sounds like ding-dong,
Moo,
Ah-tchew,
And hymns from church to name a few.

There comes a pause of purest silence,
No shame,
No tears,
No pain,
No violence.
The clouds above appear so dull,
But this is them with hearts so full.
As air,
As rain,
As sleet,

As love in a scurry with somewhere to flow,

This passion-weather then falls as drops
And travels far until it stops.
Some of these love-flakes land as snow,
This is as far as we have to go.
For all the rest you must now know
About snow-love and how it grows.